Clues from Names

Gillian Clegg

HODDER
Wayland

An imprint of Hodder Children's Books

Editors: Katrina Maitland Smith and Marcella Forster
Designer: Joyce Chester
Cover design: Stewart Larking
Consultant: John Freeman

Front cover: *left* section of Bayeux Tapestry; *middle* signpost at
Fairbourne Heath, Kent; *right* group of children.
Title page: The yearly fair at Priddy, Somerset.
Contents page: An Anglo-Saxon man writing a book.

Acknowledgements
The author would like to thank Claire Halloways for help with the projects in this book,
also Nicholas Baker and Will Coghlan.

Picture acknowledgements
The publishers gratefully acknowledge the permission of the following
to use their photographs as illustrations in this book:
Lesley and Roy Adkins Picture Library 1, 32, 33, 34, 42; Cephas Picture Library 17
(Alain Proust), 35 left (Mick Rock); The British Library 18; Gillian Clegg 41; C.M.
Dixon 3, 12, 13, 26, 27, 40 lower; Mary Evans Picture Library 8, 9, 14, 15, 16 (Alice B.
Woodward), 18 (Overland, Norges Historie), 24 (S. Bradshaw), 25, 28, 30, 36 (R. Sands),
37 lower, 40 top, 43; Eye Ubiquitous *cover* middle (Tim Page), 29 (Paul Hutley), 35 right
(P. Thompson), 38 (A. Carroll); Joel Finler 11; Hulton Deutsch 20, 37 top; The Museum
of London 5 (Richard Sorrell); Ann Ronan Picture Library 31; H.J. Sparrow 39; Wayland
Picture Library *cover* left and right, 4, 10, 21.
The map artwork on page 6 is by Hardlines.
Symbols at the top corners of each page were drawn by John Yates.

First published in 1998 by Wayland Publishers Limited
This paperback edition published in 2003 by
Hodder Wayland, an imprint of Hodder Children's Books

© Hodder Wayland 1998

Hodder Children's Books, a division of Hodder Headline Limited
338 Euston Road, London NW1 3BH

British Library Cataloguing in Publication Data
Clegg, Gillian
Clues from Names
I. Title
929.40941
ISBN 0 7502 4346 5

Printed and bound in Hong Kong

Contents

What's in a name?

Names help us to tell people apart and to tell one place from another. They also hold important clues to our past.

Imagine how you would feel if your friends and family started to call you by a completely different name. You might feel as if you were a different person. This is because your name is an important part of who you are. Your surname is a link between you and your ancestors; it can give you clues to where they came from, what language they spoke and how they made a living. Place names are important too. The name of your town may contain information about the history of the area you live in.

This book is about first names, surnames and place names. It tells you where the names come from and what they mean. There isn't enough space to mention every name. If your name, or the name of where you live, is not included, look for it in one of the books listed on page 45. You can find these through a bookshop or in a library.

The history of names
Although there were people living in Britain and Ireland many thousands of years ago, we don't know anything about the language they spoke or the names they used until about 2,500 years ago. The Celts were living in Britain at this time. They came from Central Europe, bringing their language and culture with them. The Greeks called the Celts the *Prettanoi*, meaning tattooed people, because they often painted their bodies. When the Romans invaded, they changed this to *Britannica*, which is where the name Britain comes from.

Many people and places today have names that come from Celtic words, particularly in Ireland, Scotland, Wales and Cornwall. The Welsh language, and the Gaelic language of Ireland and parts of Scotland, are Celtic languages.

When the Romans invaded England in AD 43, they brought their own language, Latin. They gave Latin endings to some English place names. For example, Lindo, the old name for Lincoln in Lincolnshire, became Lindum.

Saxons began to invade and settle in England in the fourth and fifth centuries AD. The Saxons were groups of people who came from the parts of northern Europe we now know as Denmark,

◄ Many surnames tell us what our ancestors did for a living. This medieval painting shows masons at work building a tower. Mason is a common surname.

▲ The Romans called London *Londinium*. This is what London might have looked like in Roman times.

A stone carving showing two Anglo-Saxon people. The Saxons came to England looking for new land to farm. ▶

Germany, Holland and France. The Saxon language took over from the Celtic language in England, becoming known as Anglo-Saxon. It is the basis of the English language we speak today. The Angles were a group of Saxons and England means 'land of the Angles'.

In the ninth, tenth and eleventh centuries, the Vikings (or Norsemen) invaded from Denmark and Norway. They named places in the regions where they settled, and brought their own first names. Many Vikings shared the same name, so they often had a nickname – like Red Beard – to tell people apart. These nicknames were the start of surnames.

Time chart

Date	Events	Changes to names
Before 6th century BC		People speak an unknown language.
6th and 5th centuries BC	Celts arrive in Britain and Ireland.	Celtic words used for names of people and places.
1st century AD	Romans invade and conquer England in AD 43.	Romans add their own endings to Celtic place names. Some names are written down.
5th century	Saxons settle in England.	Anglo-Saxon language known as Old English replaces Celtic in England. Saxons name many places and have their own first names (e.g. Alfred).
9th century	Vikings settle in parts of Britain and Ireland.	Vikings name places in their own language (e.g. Kirkby). They add extra names to first names.

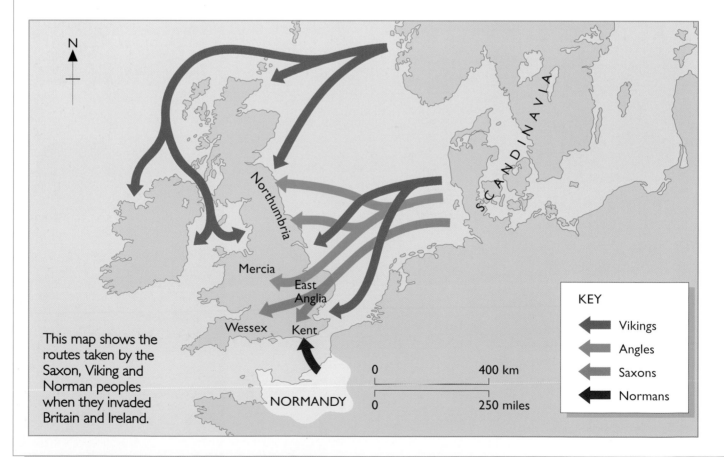

This map shows the routes taken by the Saxon, Viking and Norman peoples when they invaded Britain and Ireland.

KEY
- Vikings
- Angles
- Saxons
- Normans

SCANDINAVIA

Northumbria
Mercia
East Anglia
Wessex
Kent
NORMANDY

0   400 km
0   250 miles

Date	Events	Changes to names
10th century		Clan names in Ireland start to become surnames.
11th century	Normans invade and conquer England in 1066.	Normans bring their own first names (e.g. William), often with an extra name added. They name some places. Place names are written down in the *Domesday Book*.
12th–15th centuries		People use first names from the Bible (e.g. Mary).
16th century	Parish registers kept.	Most English people now have surnames.
	Union of England and Wales in 1536.	Welsh encouraged to take surnames.
	Reformation.	England breaks away from the Catholic Church. First names from the Old Testament of the Bible become popular (e.g. Hannah).
17th century	Union of Scottish and English royal houses in 1603 under King James VI of Scotland and I of England.	
	Plantation of Ulster.	Scots and English settle in Northern Ireland and name places.
	Huguenot refugees from France settle in England.	Huguenots bring new surnames (e.g. Cazalet).
18th century	Scottish clans are broken up.	Highland Scots now use surnames.
19th century	Industrial Revolution.	New towns are built for factory workers.
	People from Ireland and Scotland settle in England.	Irish and Scottish bring new surnames to England (e.g. McCarthy).
	Jewish immigrants settle in Britain.	Jews bring new surnames to Britain (e.g. Cohen).
20th century	New Town Movement.	Thirty-one new towns built (e.g. Telford).
	People from the Caribbean, Asia and Africa settle in Britain.	African and Asian settlers bring new first names (e.g. Usha) and surnames (e.g. Patel).

Clues from Names

In 1066, the Normans from France conquered England. They brought their own first names (Richard and William are Norman names). Like the Vikings, they didn't have many first names, so they added a second name to avoid confusing one person with another. The Normans did not name many places because they were more interested in building castles than towns and villages.

During the Middle Ages (1066–1485), everybody in England (but not in Wales or Scotland) began to have a surname as well as a first name. At that time, the Christian religion became firmly established, so many first names were taken from the Bible.

For hundreds of years, people from many other countries have been coming to live in Britain, bringing with them new surnames and first names. The Huguenots came from France in the seventeenth century, and Jews came in the nineteenth century.

Since 1945, Asians from Pakistan and India, and Africans from the Caribbean and West Africa have settled in Britain. The names of Asian and African people are beginning to be used for street names and housing estates.

How Eborakon became York

Eborakon was the Celtic name for the city in North Yorkshire now known as York. Eborakon means 'place with yew trees'. When the Romans built a fort there, they gave the Celtic name a Latin ending, so it became Eburacum. When the Saxons arrived, they looked for the closest word in their own language and turned it into Eoforwic, which means 'boar village'. Then the Vikings conquered it and called it first Evorvik, then Jorvik (pronounced 'Yorvik'). Later people changed the 'J' to a 'Y' and left out the 'vi' – hence, York.

◀ An engraving of the City of York showing how it looked in the eighteenth century. York contains many Roman, Anglo-Saxon and Viking remains.

Why names change

Names change over time because language changes. Some words are gradually dropped from the language and new ones are invented. The way people pronounce words changes too, as does the way words are spelled.

Until quite recently, most people couldn't read or write. The only time their name was written down was usually when a birth, death or marriage was being registered – or if they came within the clutches of the law!

They could not tell the priests and clerks who wrote down their name how it was spelled, so it was written as it sounded. This is why spellings differed so much.

The names of places were not written down until chronicles were kept. The most important document for discovering the early spelling of names is the *Domesday Book*. This was compiled in 1086 on the orders of William I, the Norman king who conquered England. He wanted a record of the places and property in England so

he could charge people taxes. The Norman clerks had trouble spelling some of the Saxon names so they altered them to suit themselves. Nottingham in Nottinghamshire is an example of a name changed by the Normans – the Saxons called it *Snottingham* (which means 'place of Snot's people').

▼ Shrewsbury in Shropshire. The name was first written down as *Scrobbesbyrig* in 1016. It then went through the spellings *Sciropesberie*, *Salopesberia*, *Shrobesbury* and *Shovesbury* before it became Shrewsbury. The name means 'fortified place by scrubland'.

First names

Our first names come from many different languages, some of them never spoken in Britain or Ireland.

In Britain and Ireland a first name is usually called a Christian name because it is the name you are given when you are christened. It is also known as a forename, a given name or a baptismal name.

In some countries, the personal name you are given is not the first of your names. In China, your family surname comes first and your personal name is last, though Chinese people living in Britain usually change the order. Muslim people often have a Muslim title, like Mohammed (the name of their Prophet), before their personal name.

At one time in Britain and Ireland it was quite common to give the same name to more than one child in the family. It must have been very confusing to have two brothers called John, for example. In the past, names we now think of as being for boys, such as Simon and Eustace, were also used for girls. Florence was a common name for boys. Today, Sikh people use the same names for boys and girls.

▼ People of many different backgrounds and religions have settled in Britain over the centuries, giving us a wide range of first names.

How names are chosen

Most first names are chosen not because of what they mean but because parents like the sound of them. Or they name their child after a relative or someone they admire, or because the name is in fashion. If the meaning of a name was really important it is unlikely that so many girls would be called Rebecca. This was the most popular girl's name in England and Wales in 1993 and probably means a heifer (a young cow) or a noose!

Sometimes children are named after a member of the royal family, a film or pop star, or a sportsperson. Many children born in the twentieth century were called Victoria (meaning 'victory') after the British queen. Wayne (someone who makes or drives wagons) has only been used as a first name since 1940. It became popular because it was the surname of the actor John Wayne, the star of many cowboy films. But John Wayne's real name was actually Marion Robert Morrison!

▲ The man on the right in the foreground is film star, John Wayne. Wayne was a surname meaning 'maker of wagons' and was not used as a first name until John Wayne became successful.

Names are sometimes chosen because of events: in April 1994, South Africa held its first election, in which people of all races could vote for the government of the country. The first three children to be born in one black township in Johannesburg the next day were called Freedom, Happiness and Thankful.

Clues from Names

The languages of first names

Our first names come from very many languages: from the people who have settled in Britain over the centuries; from Hebrew, Aramaic and Greek, which are the languages of the Bible; and from classical writings.

George, David, Andrew and Patrick are the names of the patron saints of England, Wales, Scotland and Ireland, respectively. We might think that these are truly British names, but not one comes from a language ever spoken in Britain. George (meaning 'farmer') and Andrew (manly) both come from Greek, David (beloved) comes from Hebrew, and Patrick (nobleman) is from the Latin word *patricius*.

Names from Celtic words are still common today, particularly in Ireland, Scotland and Wales. Some well-known Celtic names are Barry (spear), Dermot (free of envy), Deirdre (one who rages) and Olwen (white track).

▼ St. George, the patron saint of England, killing a dragon. This picture was painted on a wall of the church in Pickering, Yorkshire in the fifteenth century.

John

This Hebrew name comes from the Bible and means 'favoured by God'. St. John the Baptist and St. John the Evangelist are important Christian figures in the Bible, and many parents have named their children after them. John has been one of the most common names in Christian countries since the twelfth century.

There are many different spellings and variations of John. Ian is a Scottish version; Eoin, Sean and Shane are Irish versions; and Ioan and Evan are Welsh. Ivan, Jean, Hans, Giovanni and Juan all mean the same as John in other countries.

Nicknames and short names for John include Jack, Jock, Jan and Jen. Female versions of John include Jane, Jean, Janet, Joanna, Sinead, Siobhan and Shona.

Lots of surnames come from John too. Two common ones are Jones and Evans.

▲ St. John the Evangelist, one of the twelve apostles of Jesus Christ, and the writer of the Gospel According to St. John in the Bible.

Some Anglo-Saxon first names survive as surnames, such as Godwin (good friend) and Sweetlove, which means what it says.

The Chinese naming system is similar to the Anglo-Saxon. They also choose names made up of more than one word. Typical words used in boys' names are Tai (healthy) and Chiang (strong). Ying (flower) and Li (beautiful) are popular for girls.

When the Vikings came to Britain and Ireland, they brought some new first names, such as Eric (ruler) and Ralph (counsel wolf). Viking children were often given the same first name as their parents or grandparents, so people had to use nicknames to make it clear who was who. Some of these names were quite insulting, meaning drunkard, idler, short leg or clumsy!

The Normans did not have many different names. Emma (whole, universal), William (stout, helmet), Alice (noble) and Richard (stern, ruler) are Norman names we still use today.

When the Anglo-Saxons first settled in England, people only had one name (there were no surnames) so it was important to make that name as individual as possible. Anglo-Saxon names were usually made up of two separate words. The words did not always make sense when put together. Often a name consisted of one syllable from the name of each parent. For example, a man called Alfred (which means 'elf counsel') and a woman called Edith (meaning 'happy' and 'war') might name their son Aldith. Other Anglo-Saxon names like this that we still use today are Audrey ('noble' and 'might') and Edward ('happy' and 'protector').

When the Normans arrived, people stopped using many of the Anglo-Saxon names, although some became popular again in the eighteenth and nineteenth centuries.

Clues from Names

Biblical names

During the Middle Ages, the Christian Church encouraged people to name their children after saints and other important people in the New Testament of the Bible. This meant that names taken from the Hebrew and Greek languages became common. Some examples are Matthew (gift of God), Philip (lover of horses), Peter (stone, rock), Barbara (foreigner) and Mary (from the Hebrew name, Miriam, though no one is quite sure what it means; Mariam, the Muslim version of Mary is said to mean 'pure').

Jesus, the most famous name in the Bible, has never been used as a first name in Britain and Ireland, although it is quite common in Spanish-speaking countries. It means 'God protects'. Joshua and Jason are thought to mean the same.

Different names were taken from the Bible in sixteenth-century England, when the Church of England broke away from the Roman Catholic Church.

▲ During the Reformation in the 16th century, King Henry VIII replaced the Pope as head of the church in England. This led to England becoming a Protestant country.

This change was known as the Reformation. The people of England were encouraged to dislike all things Catholic and the names of the saints went out of use for a time. People took names from the Old Testament of the Bible instead. Names that became popular after the Reformation include Benjamin (son of the right hand), Jonathan (God has given), Sarah or Sara (princess) and Hannah (God has favoured). Ann, Anne, Annette and Anita come from Hannah, though both Ann and Anne were in use before the Reformation.

14

The Puritans were a very strict religious group of the seventeenth century. They thought that Biblical names were not pure enough for their children, so they called them names like Patience, Faith, Hope and Charity – or even Obedience, Fear-Not and Sorry-for-Sin. Some of these names are still in use.

Surnames and place names as first names

After the Reformation, surnames started to be used as first names. Often a mother's surname would be given to her child between the first name and surname. For example, Mary Kelly and John Ferguson called their daughter Sara Kelly Ferguson. Eventually many of these surnames became first names, for example Curtis (courteous), Craig (someone who lived near a rock), and Kelly, which means 'strife'.

The names of places were used as first names too. Winston (Wine's village), Ashley (place near an ash wood) and Shirley (bright clearing) are examples of this.

Tracy/Tracey

Here's a name with a complicated story. It was a place name, a surname and a boy's name before it became a girl's name. There was a place in France called Traci-Bocage. A family from there settled in Bovey, in Devon, in 1219 and gave themselves the surname Tracy. Tracy was used as a first name from the nineteenth century. One of the male characters in Charles Dickens's *Pickwick Papers*, written in 1836, is called Tracy Tupman. As a girl's name, it was probably a short name for Teresa. It only became really popular as a girl's name in the 1960s after the release of the film *High Society*, in which the heroine was called Tracy Samantha.

▼ The kneeling man is Tracy Tupman from Charles Dickens's novel *The Pickwick Papers*. He is shown here with two other characters, Miss Wardle and the Fat Boy.

Clues from Names

Flower and jewel names
At the end of the nineteenth century, it became fashionable to call girls after flowers, such as Violet, Daisy, Pansy and Poppy. Some much older names come from flowers too, such as Susan (lily), Eirlys (snowdrop) and Blodwen (white flower).

Then the fashion turned to jewels – Ruby, Opal, Crystal, Amber, Beryl, Coral, Jade, Gemma (Italian for 'gem') and Pearl were used as first names. Margaret means pearl too, but it was also the name of a saint and has been used for much longer. Other names meaning pearl are the Hindu name, Moti, and the Muslim name, Durrah.

Wendy, Vanessa and Lorna

These names were made up by writers and don't mean anything!

Wendy was invented by J. M. Barrie who wrote the play *Peter Pan* in 1904. Barrie had a friend who always called him 'friend', and the friend's daughter nicknamed him 'friendy-wendy'. He obviously liked it, as he decided to use the name Wendy for the heroine of his play.

The seventeenth- and eighteenth-century writer, Jonathan Swift, made up the name of Vanessa for his friend, Esther Vanhomrigh, using parts of her real name.

Lorna comes from the child heroine of R. D. Blackmore's 1869 novel, *Lorna Doone*. It is probably from the name of a place in Scotland: Lorne, in Argyll.

▶ Wendy kissing Peter Pan in J. M. Barrie's play *Peter Pan*.

Other types of first name

As well as flowers and jewels, animals and birds are used as names. Rachel means 'ewe'; Deborah and Melissa both mean 'bee'; Malcolm, Jemima and Colum all mean 'dove'; Giles means 'young goat'; and Marlon means 'blackbird'.

Some names originally described a person's appearance or character. There are colours of hair or skin: Donald (brown); Blanche (white); Melanie, Kieran and Krishna (black); and Lloyd (grey). Other names describe what faces or hair look like. Crispin, for example, means 'curled hair'; Simon, 'snub-nosed'; Hasan, 'handsome'; and Lalita, 'beautiful'. Some names describe what people were or how they behaved. Francis means 'a Frenchman'; Thomas, 'a twin'; Amin, 'reliable'; Ayesha, 'prosperous'; Farah, 'cheerful'; and Dapta means 'proud'.

Children are sometimes named after the month in which they are born: April, May and June are the most popular. Others might be named after festivals: Noël and

▲ The following names all mean 'lion': Leo, Lionel, Asad (a Muslim name); Agu, Simba and Usamah (all African names).

Natalie both come from *natalis*, the Latin word for 'Day of Birth'.

African children are often given the name of the day of the week on which they were born. If an Ashanti child is born on a Monday, it could be called Kwadwo if it is a boy or Adwoa if it is a girl. Some names show the order in which a child was born. Pili means 'the second child'; Taiwo, 'the eldest of twins'. Other African first names mean quite complicated things. Owodunni means 'it is nice to have money'; Kufo means 'father shares the birth pains'!

Illuminated letters

The writing in this picture is from medieval times. It has 'illuminated' capital letters. Before the printing press was invented, books were handwritten by monks, who often illustrated letters with patterns or pictures.

Try writing your name with an illuminated first letter, or make a birthday card for a friend with the first letter of your friend's name illuminated on the front. See if you can think of a decoration that illustrates the meaning of your friend's name.

Top twenty first names for boys (England and Wales)

1800	1900	1950	1985	1996
1 William	1 William	1 David	1 Christopher	1 Jack
2 John	2 John	2 John	2 Matthew	2 Daniel
3 Thomas	3 George	3 Peter	3 David	3 Thomas
4 James	4 Thomas	4 Michael	4 James	4 James
5 George	5 Charles	5 Alan	5 Daniel	5 Joshua
6 Joseph	6 Frederick	6 Robert	6 Andrew	6 Matthew
7 Richard	7 Arthur	7 Stephen	7 Steven	7 Ryan
8 Henry	8 James	8 Paul	8 Michael	8 Samuel
9 Robert	9 Albert	9 Brian	9 Mark	9 Joseph
10 Charles	10 Ernest	10 Graham	10 Paul	10 Liam
11 Samuel	11 Robert	11 Philip	11 Richard	11 Luke
12 Edward	12 Henry	12 Anthony	12 Adam	12 Jordan
13 Benjamin	13 Alfred	13 Colin	13 Robert	13 Connor
14 Isaac	14 Sidney	14 Christopher	14 Lee	14 Alexander
15 Peter	15 Joseph	15 Geoffrey	15 Craig	15 Benjamin
16 Daniel	16 Harold	16 William	16 Benjamin	16 Adam
17 David	17 Harry	17 James	17 Thomas	17 Jake
18 Francis	18 Frank	18 Keith	18 Peter	18 Harry
19 Stephen	19 Walter	19 Terence	19 Anthony	19 William
20 Jonathan	20 Herbert	20 Barry	20 Shaun	20 Michael

First name fashions

How many people do you know called Ethel, Ada, Arthur or Ernest? You might know one or two, or none at all. If you had been born 100 years ago, you might have known several. Like clothes, names go in and out of fashion, particularly names for girls. New names are introduced and old names dropped, or used only as second names, until the cycle goes right round and they become popular again.

The lists below show the top twenty boys' and girls' names in England and Wales for the years 1800, 1900, 1950, 1985 and 1996. You will see that names like Daniel (which means 'God has judged'), Benjamin, Richard, Sarah, Hannah, Charlotte and Rebecca appear in the 1800 list but not in the 1900 or 1950 list, then appear again in 1985 and 1996. Fashion in girls' names changes more quickly than fashion in boys' names. Favourite names for boys, like James and Robert, appear on all or most of the lists but not one of the top twenty names for girls in 1950 is on the 1996 list.

Fashion is set by parents who give their children unusual names. If they have chosen a good name, other people will copy them. But fashions in names don't last very long.

Top twenty first names for girls (England and Wales)

1800	1900	1950	1985	1996
1 Mary	1 Florence	1 Susan	1 Sarah	1 Sophie
2 Ann	2 Mary	2 Linda	2 Claire	2 Jessica
3 Elizabeth	3 Alice	3 Christine	3 Emma	3 Chloe
4 Sarah	4 Annie	4 Margaret	4 Laura	4 Emily
5 Jane	5 Elsie	5 Carol	5 Rebecca	5 Lauren
6 Hannah	6 Edith	6 Jennifer	6 Gemma	6 Rebecca
7 Susan	7 Elizabeth	7 Janet	7 Rachel	7 Charlotte
8 Martha	8 Doris	8 Patricia	8 Kelly	8 Hannah
9 Margaret	9 Dorothy	9 Barbara	9 Victoria	9 Amy
10 Charlotte	10 Ethel	10 Ann	10 Katherine	10 Megan
11 Harriet	11 Gladys	11 Sandra	11 Katie	11 Shannon
12 Betty	12 Lilian	12 Pamela	12 Nicola	12 Katie
13 Maria	13 Hilda	13 Pauline	13 Jennifer	13 Emma
14 Catherine	14 Margaret	14 Jean	14 Natalie	14 Bethany
15 Frances	15 Winifred	15 Jacqueline	15 Hayley	15 Lucy
16 Mary Ann	16 Lily	16 Kathleen	16 Michelle	16 Laura
17 Nancy	17 Ellen	17 Sheila	17 Amy	17 Georgia
18 Rebecca	18 Ada	18 Valerie	18 Lisa	18 Sarah
19 Alice	19 Emily	19 Maureen	19 Lindsay	19 Jade
20 Ellen	20 Violet	20 Gillian	20 Samantha	20 Abigail

Surnames

Surnames are an important link with our ancestors. Your surname may tell you the first name of one of your ancestors, where your ancestors came from, how they earned their living or what they were like.

The word surname comes from the French word *surnom*; this comes from the Latin words *supra nomen*, meaning 'an extra name'. The first surnames came from clan names. Clans were groups of families in Ireland and Scotland. They added the name of the clan after their first name. In other parts of the British Isles, people with common first names were given extra names to make it easier to tell them apart. These extra names were really nicknames.

Clan names started to become surnames in Ireland from about the tenth century, but it wasn't until about 1500 that most people in England and the Lowlands of Scotland had family names that were passed from parents to children. It was another 100 years or so before people in Wales took surnames. In the Highlands of Scotland, clan names didn't become surnames until the eighteenth century.

▼ Members of the MacLean clan gathering together at Duart Castle, Isle of Mull. Clans are groups of people who share the same name and the same ancestors.

▲ A scene from the Bayeux Tapestry showing Norman soldiers sailing across the English Channel in 1066 to invade Britain.

The practice of giving people extra names increased dramatically after the Normans invaded England. The Normans did not have many different first names, so it was difficult to tell people apart. Adding surnames made it easier to identify people. They also became important for inheritance. If a landowner wanted to make sure that his property would pass to his eldest son when he died, it was important that his son was known by the same name.

As the population grew, especially between the twelfth and fifteenth centuries, more and more extra names came into use. It was probably in 1538, when parish registers were ordered to be kept for recording births, deaths and marriages, that it became the normal practice to pass names from parents to children.

Surnames have many possible origins. Your surname might be the first name or the nickname of one of your ancestors, or the name of the town or village your family came from. It could be a feature of the landscape where one of your ancestors lived or what one of your ancestors did for a living.

We don't know exactly what many surnames mean, so we often have to guess. Some surnames could mean several different things. The name Warren, for example, could come from a place called Warenne in France, or from the first name Warin, or because someone once lived by a rabbit warren! The only way to find out which is the right meaning for your name is to trace your family history and see how the name was first written down.

Clues from Names

Surnames from first names

If your surname starts with Fitz- or ends in -son or -s, the chances are that the rest of your name was the first name of one of your ancestors. Fitzalan would originally have been the son of Alan; Johnson, the son of John; and Williams, the son of William. Fitz- comes from *fils de*, the French for 'son of'. Adding an *s* to the end of a first name is a way of shortening the Saxon word son. (Not all surnames ending in -son are from first names, however. Mason means a skilled stone worker.)

Mac is the word for son in the Celtic languages spoken in Ireland and Scotland. Many names starting with Mac- or Mc- are followed by a personal name, like McHugh (son of Hugh). There are other Mac-names that mean different things, like McIntosh, which means 'son of the chief'. Under English rule, many Celtic names in Scotland and Ireland were anglicized. MacFergus, for instance, became Ferguson; MacOwen became Keown or Cowan.

A lot of Irish names begin with O', like O'Neill and O'Brien. This means 'descendant of', rather than 'son of'. The Welsh word for son is *ap*. This has become part of some names. Ap Richard (son of Richard) became Pritchard, Ap Hugh became Pugh, and Ap Owen became Bowen.

Family tree

Write down your surname, your mother's surname and all the other surnames in your family – your grandmothers', grandfathers', great grandmothers', great grandfathers' – as far back as possible. Make a family tree like this one. Can you find out what the names mean?

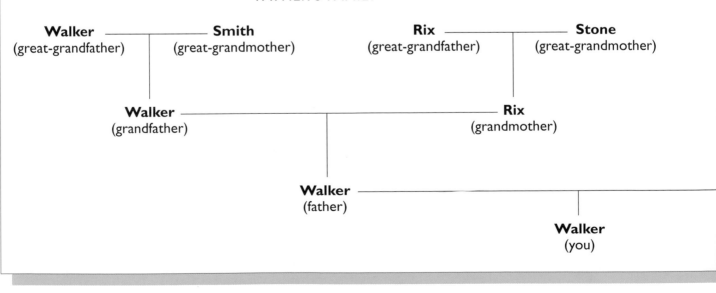

FATHER'S FAMILY

Walker (great-grandfather) —— **Smith** (great-grandmother) **Rix** (great-grandfather) —— **Stone** (great-grandmother)

Walker (grandfather) —————————— **Rix** (grandmother)

Walker (father) ————

Walker (you)

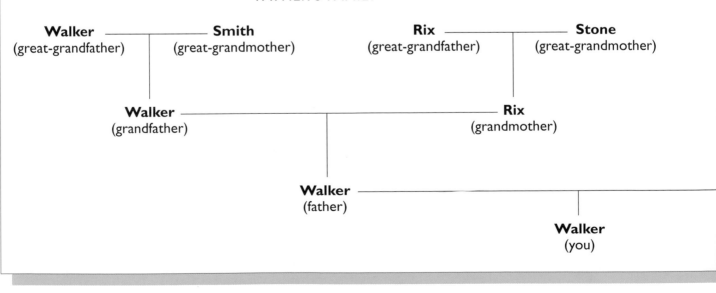

22

Some first names have become surnames without any additions, such as Paul or Patrick, and sometimes different endings, like -cock, -et, or -kin, were added to a first name to make a surname.

Today's surnames show us what first names people were being given in the eleventh to sixteenth centuries, when surnames were being introduced. Many of these first names are still used today: Adam, from which we get surnames like Addams, Adcock and Atkins; and Walter, from which come Walters, Watt and Watkins. Some of the original first names are no longer used. The surnames Payne and Pane are from the Old French first name Paien (meaning 'pagan').

First names like Richard, Robert and William were so common that people with these names were often called by a short name to tell them apart. These short names have given us surnames too. Short names for Richard were Rick, Ric, Dick or Hick. Surnames from these names include Ricks, Ricketts, Dix, Dickens, Hitchcock and Hiskell. Hick was sometimes changed to Higg, giving the surnames Higgs, Higgins and Higson.

Girls' first names have become surnames too. Marriott comes from Mary; Mabbs means 'son of Mabel'; Maggs, 'son of Margaret'; Tillotson, 'son of Matilda'.

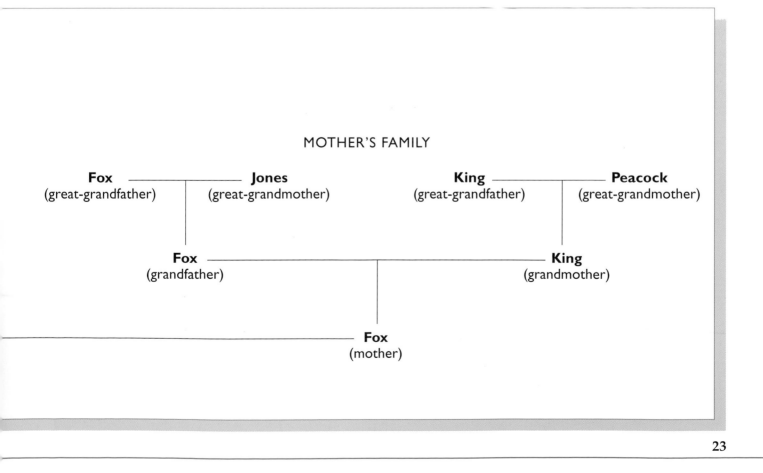

MOTHER'S FAMILY

Fox (great-grandfather) — **Jones** (great-grandmother)

King (great-grandfather) — **Peacock** (great-grandmother)

Fox (grandfather) — **King** (grandmother)

Fox (mother)

Surnames from names of places

This type of surname usually (but not always) ends with a word like -ham, -ton or -by (generally meaning village – see box on pages 34–5). Many more English surnames come from names of places than do Welsh, Scottish or Irish surnames.

A place-name surname might give you a clue to where your family came from, but there are problems with this. Many places in different parts of the country had the same name – there are a lot of places called Ashby and Newton, for example – and other places have disappeared. Surnames have also changed over the years, which can make the original place name difficult to recognize. The surname Wooster, for example, is from the place name Worcester.

English, Scott, Irish and Welsh (or Walsh, Welch) are quite common surnames, and they mean what they say. Less easy to recognize, however, are surnames such as Dench, which means someone from Denmark; Gascoigne, someone from the French area of Gascony; and Fleming, from Flanders, a province in Belgium.

Some English surnames come from the names of places in France: Beecham comes from a place called Beauchamp, Percy from Perci-en-Auger, and Ross from Rots. These are places from which the Norman invaders came.

Kendal, Kendall, Kendell, Kendle

All these surnames come from the name of the town of Kendal in Cumbria. Kendal means 'valley of the River Kent'.

Before the Industrial Revolution in the nineteenth century, people didn't usually move very far from the place where they were born, so most place-name surnames tended to be found around the place after which they were named. But the Kendal names are unusual: they are found in many parts of the country from the fifteenth century onwards. This is probably because Kendal produced a woollen cloth which was sold all over the country by traders, some of whom decided to settle elsewhere.

◄ A view of Kendal in Cumbria in 1832.

If your surname is from a French place name, however, it does not necessarily mean that your ancestors arrived with William the Conqueror. People working on the estates owned by the Normans often used the landowner's surname.

Surnames from features in the landscape

When surnames were introduced, most villages were very small and probably home to only a few families. As places grew in size, a person might be given a name indicating exactly where they lived in the village – by the brook (which gives us the surname, Brooks), up the hill (Hill), near the wood (Wood), or at the edge of the village or town (Townsend).

Once we know this, it is easy to see what names like Ford, Heath, Lake, Marsh and Banks mean. However, some come from words no longer used, such as Slade (a valley), Crouch (near a cross), Rhodes (a clearing in the forest) and Botham (the bottom of a valley). Sidebotham means 'wide valley', and the meaning of Shufflebotham is 'valley with a stream for washing sheep'.

In the twelfth and thirteenth centuries, the words *atte, atten* (which mean 'at the', 'over', 'by', 'beneath') and *de, de la, du* (French for 'of the') were often used before a name. A man named James atte Feld, for example, lived in Sussex in 1296. These extra words were dropped from most names by 1500 but sometimes were joined up with the name, as in Atfield (at the field), Delafield (of the field), Inwood (in the wood) and Nash (from atten ash – at the ash tree).

◄ Sir Winston Churchill, Prime Minister of Britain during the Second World War. His surname means 'church hill'.

25

Clues from Names

Surnames from occupations

This type of surname may tell you how an ancestor earned a living. Many occupation names end in -er, such as Baker, Butcher, Carpenter. It is obvious what these mean because we still use the same names for these trades today. However, you might not know what people with the following common surnames did for a living: Baxter (a female baker), Chandler (a maker and seller of candles), Fletcher (maker and trader of arrows), Frobisher (a polisher of armour), Genner (an engineer), Jagger (a driver of carts), Ripper (a basket maker) and Walker (a cloth worker). Farmer did not mean what it does today; a farmer was a tax collector. A person who farmed land was known as an ackerman.

Since surnames developed in the Middle Ages, occupation surnames tell us a lot about medieval life. Here are some names that don't end in -er: Chapman (a seller of cheap goods – a peddler),

▲ A medieval butcher in France cutting up a pig. In England his surname may have been Kellogg 'kill hog' (pigs were also known as hogs and swine).

Clark/e (a clerk or secretary), Kellogg (literally 'kill hog' – a slaughterer of pigs), Leach or Leech (a doctor), Steadman (someone who looked after horses), Ward (a guard or watchman) and Wright (a workman who made things, usually in wood).

Occupation surnames were not as common in Scotland, Ireland and Wales as in England, but there were some. Hickey was a doctor; Scully, a scholar; Lamond or Lamont, a lawman; McIntyre, the son of a carpenter; and McPherson, the son of a parson.

If your name is Bailey, Baillie, Reeve, Sheriff or Sumner, you probably had an ancestor who was an official in medieval times.

26

Biddle, Beadle or Beadnell mean your ancestor was a beadle (a town crier). Catchpole means catch fowl, an official who seized poultry from people who couldn't pay their debts.

Some occupation surnames show people's position in society. In medieval times, serfs or slaves were at the lower level, lords at the top and many other classes in between. The surname Bond means a bonded man – a slave. The surnames Freebody, Freeborn and Freeman mean someone who was not a slave. Franklin means a gentleman (but not a nobleman). Lord means landowner, though sometimes it would have been a nickname for someone who acted in a lordly fashion!

If your name is Kemp, your ancestor was a warrior or an athlete. The name Palmer means your ancestor made an important journey, called a pilgrimage, to the Holy Lands and came back with a branch of palm to prove it!

Smith

In medieval times, every village had its own smith who made iron objects such as shoes for horses, tools and weapons. It is not surprising, then, that the surname Smith has become the most common name in England, Scotland and the USA.

Smith comes from the Old English word *smid* and is one of the oldest names known. An Ecceard Smith is recorded as long ago as AD 975. Over the generations, the name has given rise to many different versions, such as Smyth, Smithers and Smithson.

Other surnames also mean smith. Gow and Gowan come from *gobha* and *ghobhainn*, the Scottish and Irish words for smith. Goff and Gough come from the Welsh *gof* and the Cornish *gov*, both meaning smith. Faber is Latin for smith, and Farrar, Ferrar, Fearon and Farrier come from the Old French word *ferreor*, which means working with iron.

▼ This thirteenth century wood carving shows a smith forging a sword in his smithy.

Surnames from nicknames

People have always been given nicknames. They are still used today, even though we do not need them to tell one person from another. It is not surprising to find that many nicknames have been passed on as surnames. In Viking times, if there were two people in a village called Eric, for example, one might have been known as Eric the Red because of the colour of his hair or face. Later the name would have become Eric Read, Reed or Reid. The other might have been called Eric the Bald because he had no hair. Later his surname would have become Ball or Ballard.

Many nicknames describe appearance and colouring. Obvious ones are White, Brown and Grey. Others that are harder to recognize are Boyd (yellow hair), Cave (bald), Cooney (handsome), Fairfax (beautiful hair), Hoare (grey hair), Long (a tall person) and Smollett (someone with a small head).

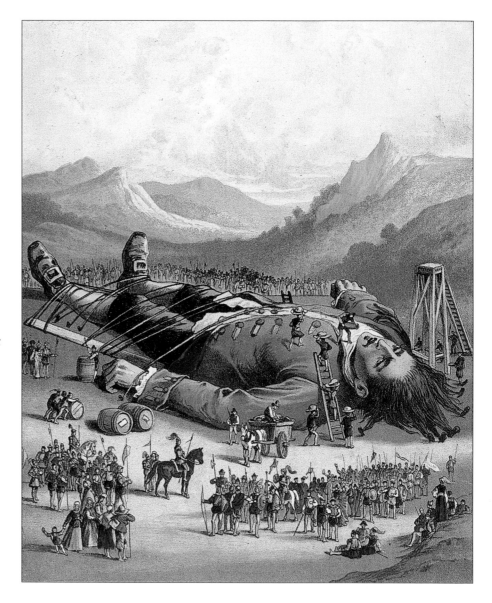

▲ Lemuel Gulliver, the hero of *Gulliver's Travels* by Jonathan Swift. Here Gulliver wakes up to discover he has been captured by the people of Lilliput, who are only 15 cm tall. The name Gulliver means 'glutton' – someone who likes their food too much!

Some nicknames are not very polite. Campbell means 'crooked mouth'; Cameron, 'crooked nose'; Cruickshank, 'bow-legged'; Giffard, 'chubby cheeks'; Kennedy, 'ugly head'; and Pauncefoot, 'round belly'.

Other nickname surnames tell us something about the character of the first people to have these names. Dempsey means 'proud'; Docherty, 'the stern one'; Gotobed, 'lazy'; Merryweather, 'cheerful'; Moody, 'brave'; Pennyfather, 'a miser'; Smart, 'active'; and Parfitt, 'perfect'. Wiseman was a name given to magicians – and sometimes fools as well!

The names of animals and birds have also been taken as surnames. Common examples are Bull, Lamb, Wolf, Fox, Dove, Finch, Peacock and Raven. Even fish names such as Bass, Tench and Chubb have been used. No one really knows why these types of names were adopted. Perhaps the person who originally took an animal name had qualities that were associated with that animal: the fox has traditionally been seen as cunning, the peacock as proud. Perhaps the person looked like the animal!

Surnames also come from expressions people use: Bongers is from *bonjour*, the French for 'good day'; Purdy and Purdew come from the French *pour Dieu*, which means 'by God'.

Local names

Many people living in the same area tend to have the same surname. Go with an adult to a graveyard or cemetery near your home and copy down names from about fifty gravestones. Or you can look in old local newspapers for the names of people who have died over the years. Which name is most common and what does it mean?

▲ The grave of writer, Anne Brontë, in Scarborough, Yorkshire. Anne's father's surname was really Brunty, but he changed it to Brontë.

Clues from Names

Other surnames

There are too many people with names like Prince and King for them all to be descended from royalty. These names, and surnames such as Bishop and Abbott, may have been taken by servants of royalty or church officials. They may be nicknames for people who behaved like a king or a bishop, or for those who acted such parts in the pageants and plays that were so popular in the Middle Ages.

Many Celtic names don't fall into any of the categories described above. Murphy, the most common name in Ireland, means 'sea warrior'. Duffy means 'black man of peace'.

People who have come to live in Britain from other countries have brought new surnames.

In the late seventeenth century, Protestants from France, called Huguenots, fled to Britain to escape being persecuted by the Catholics. They had French names like Bosanquet (dwarf) and Cazalet (good house site).

▼ St. Bartholomew's Day Massacre, France, in 1572. The Huguenots, who were Protestants, are being murdered by the Catholics. Can you see the bodies floating in the river?

Many Jewish people settled in Britain in the nineteenth century. Although Jews had lived in Britain centuries before, they were expelled in 1290 – before surnames were really developed – and were not allowed back until 1655. Cohen, for example, is Hebrew for 'priest'.

People from the Caribbean often have English-sounding surnames. This is usually because their eighteenth-century African ancestors were taken to the Caribbean islands as slaves by the British. The slaves were either given a name by their employer or they took their employer's name.

▲ Slaves in the Caribbean producing indigo, a blue powder that comes from a plant and which is used as a dye. The white man on the right is supervising the black slaves.

Many people of African origin are now changing back to African names.

Common Asian surnames in Britain are Khan, a Muslim name meaning ruler; Patel, a Gujerati surname meaning 'people entitled to own and farm land'; and Singh, which means 'lion'. (Singh is not really a surname since any man who is a Sikh is called Singh, but many Sikhs use Singh as their surname.) Wang (meaning 'king') is a common Chinese surname. The common Chinese surname Chang means a bowman.

The twenty most common surnames in England and Wales

1 Smith	6 Brown	11 Robinson	16 Walker
2 Jones	7 Thomas	12 Wilson	17 Hughes
3 Williams	8 Evans	13 Wright	18 Green
4 Taylor	9 Roberts	14 Wood	19 Lewis
5 Davies	10 Johnson	15 Hall	20 Edwards

Can you interpret these names? Four are occupation surnames. Which ones are they and what were the occupations? Which three are names of landscape features? Which one is a nickname-type surname? The rest are surnames from first names. What were the first names?

Place names

Place names are much older than surnames. The name of your village, town or city may tell you which invaders settled there and what it was like in the past.

▲ Allerford, Somerset, which means 'ford by the alder trees'. You can see the ford under the bridge.

Most place names are made up of two or more words. One word usually tells us what the place was at the time it was named – a farm, village, valley or river for example. The other word (or words) usually tells us what was special about the place – where it was, who it belonged to, what it looked like or what was produced there.

Stamford, in Lincolnshire, is made up of the old word *stam*, which means 'stone', and 'ford', which is a place where a river can be crossed. Musselburgh, in Lothian, means 'a fortified town (*burgh*) where mussels could be found'.

Some meanings are obvious, such as Greenhill and Newcastle, but others are made up of old words we no longer use. The box on pages 34–5 lists the most common words found in place names, the old languages from which the words come, and what they mean. Look at the box and see if you can work out the meaning of

Kirkby (Merseyside) and Chesterton (Cambridgeshire).

In the past, however, some very similar words have meant different things and modern spellings often hide this. *Ham* means 'farm' or 'village' in the names of Birmingham (West Midlands), Berkhamstead (Hertfordshire) and Hampstead (London) but not in Cookham (Berkshire) or Chippenham (Wiltshire). In the last two names, 'ham' means 'land in the bend of a river' and comes from another word, spelt *hamm*, which has now lost the second

Write a limerick

A sacked young curator from Penge
Decided to take his revenge
So out of sheer malice
He burned down Kew Palace
And wrote naughty words on Stonehenge.

This kind of poem is called a limerick. Can you write one using the name of your town? It could start like this:

There was a young girl from Dundee …

'm'. The best way to find out what the name of a place means is to discover how it was spelt when it was first written down.

▼ Muchelney, Somerset, which means 'large island'. As the land is very low here, it is frequently flooded and this village is often surrounded by water.

What place names tell us
Place names are a guide to where the different invaders of Britain and Ireland settled. The Romans, Saxons and Vikings lived mainly in England, so many places in Ireland, Wales, Cornwall and Scotland still have the names the Celts gave them.

The Romans occupied England for nearly 400 years. They gave some places new names but usually took the Celtic name and gave it an ending from their own language, Latin. After the Romans left, the Anglo-Saxons and Vikings tended to translate these names into words that sounded more like their languages.

33

Common words found in place names

Word (origin)	Meaning	Example
bally (C)	homestead	Ballycastle, County Antrim (homestead near the castle)
ben (C)	mountain	Ben More, Strathclyde (big mountain)
borne, bourne (OE)	stream	Fishbourne, Sussex (fish stream)
borough, brough, burgh, bury (OE)	fort or fortified town	Aldeburgh, Suffolk (old fort)
by (ON)	farm or village	Blaby, Lancashire (Bla's farm)
caster, cester chester (OE)	Roman fort or town	Chichester, West Sussex (Cissa's fort)
chep, chip (OE)	market	Chepstow, Gwent (market place)
clon (C)	meadow, pasture	Clonmel, Tipperary (meadow of honey)
coat, cot (OE)	cottage	Didcot, Oxfordshire (Dudda's cottage)
combe (OE)	deep or narrow valley	Babbacombe, Devon (Babba's valley)
dale, dean, den (OE, ON)	valley	Langdale, Cumbria (long valley)
don, dun (C, OE)	hill	Maldon, Essex (hill with a cross)
ey (OE)	island	Selsey, West Sussex (seal island)

KEY

C = Celtic
(language of the Celts)

L = Latin
(language of the Romans)

OE = Old English
(language of the Saxons)

ON = Old Norse
(language of the Vikings)

◄ The Roman fort at Portchester, Hampshire. Port means 'harbour'; chester means 'Roman fort'.

Place names

▲ Shaftesbury, Dorset, means fortified town that either belonged to a man called Sceaft, or is on a steep hill.

▶ Helmsley, Yorkshire, which means clearing in a wood of someone called Helm.

Word (origin)	Meaning	Example
glen (C)	valley	Glendalough, Wicklow (valley of the two lakes)
head (OE)	hill or headland	Gateshead, Tyne and Wear (hill with goats)
holt (OE)	wood	Knockholt, Kent (oak wood)
hurst (OE)	wooded hill	Crowhurst, Surrey (wooded hill with crows)
lee, leigh, ley (OE)	clearing in a wood	Barnsley, South Yorkshire (Beorn's clearing)
pont (L)	bridge	Pontefract, West Yorkshire (broken bridge)
stead, sted (OE)	place, often religious	Brasted, Kent (broad place)
stock, stoke (OE)	religious place or site, or an outlying farm	Stoke Mandeville, Buckinghamshire (place belonging to the Mandeville family)
stow (OE)	meeting place or holy place	Felixstowe, Suffolk (St. Felix's place)
thorp, thorpe (OE, ON)	farm	Scunthorpe, Humberside (Skuma's farm)
thwaite (ON)	glade or clearing	Crosthwaite, Cumbria (clearing by a cross)
ton (OE)	village or farm	Preston, Lancashire (farm belonging to priests)
wich, wick (OE)	farm or port	Keswick, Cumbria (cheese farm)
worth (OE)	enclosure, homestead	Tamworth, Staffordshire (enclosure on the River Tame)

At first the Anglo-Saxons lived mainly in southern England, where they built new settlements. Most of the place names there come from Saxon words. Viking place names are mainly found where the Vikings settled, in north and eastern England, north and west Scotland and around the coast of Ireland.

By the time the Normans arrived, most places already had a name. The Normans did name some places, however, and they must have liked their new country because many of their place names start with Beau- (*beau* is French for beautiful), like Beaulieu (beautiful place) in Hampshire. They also added another word to some places with a common name so that it was easier to tell places apart. They added Keynes after Milton in Milton Keynes, Buckinghamshire.

▼ Inverness in the Highlands of Scotland means 'mouth of the River Ness'.

Geographical names

The most ancient names of all are the names of rivers. Many river names have become the names of places: Exeter, in Devon, means 'Roman town on the River Exe'; Streams, lakes and waterfalls feature in names. Haslemere (Surrey) means 'lake among hazel trees'. Catterick (North Yorkshire) comes from *cataracta,* a Latin word for 'waterfall'.

The meaning of Blackpool in Lancashire is easy to work out (the stream that fed the black pool is now the town's main sewer). Dublin, in the Republic of Ireland, means exactly the same. It comes from the Irish words *dubh* (black) and *linn* (pool).

Words for rocks, hills, valleys, woods and trees are also used in names: Ailsa Craig (Strathclyde) means 'fairy rock'; Acle

Place names

Look at a large-scale map of your area. Write down the place where you live and the ten nearest towns and villages. Next to each name, write down what it means. You can find the meanings in a place-name dictionary in your local library if they are not in this book. You could then draw pictures of what these names mean.

Hill, hill, hill!

This is what the name Pendle Hill, in Lancashire, means. The Celts gave the place the name pen which means 'hill'. The Saxons didn't understand the Celtic language well enough to recognize its meaning and added their own word for a hill, hyll, which became -dle. Later people forgot what this meant and added another 'hill' to make it very clear that this was a hilly place!

▶ Pendle Hill seen from the village of Downham, Lancashire.

(Norfolk), 'oak wood'; Brynmawr (Gwynedd), 'big hill'; Ampthill (Bedfordshire), 'ant hill'.

▼ Cork in Ireland in the seventeenth century.

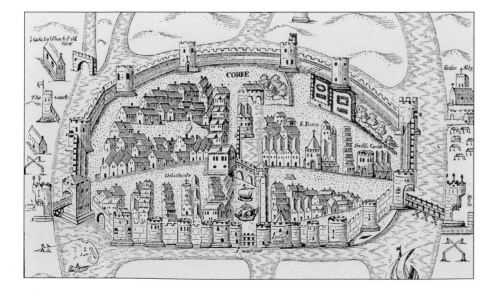

Early people were farmers, and the type and condition of the soil was important for growing crops. Some place names, therefore, tell us about the soil: Cork (County Cork) means 'marshy'; Cleethorpes (Humberside), 'hamlets in clay soil'; Auchinleck (Strathclyde), 'field of the flat stones'.

Some place names tell us about travel. There are thousands of place names ending in -ford or -bridge, for example. Broadway (Hereford and Worcester) means 'broad road' and Crossmaglen (Armagh), 'a crossroads'. Malpas (Cheshire) means 'difficult passage', while Morpeth (Northumberland) is even more sinister. It means 'path where a murder took place'!

Clues from Names

Names from trade and industry

Sometimes a place name can tell us which crops were grown or which industries were established there. Appleby (Cumbria) means 'apple farm'; Barton (Devon), 'barley farm'; Potton (Bedfordshire), 'a village where pots are made'.

Salt was very important for preserving meat through the winter before farmers were able to keep animals alive through the coldest months. The word is present in many names, like Salthouse (Norfolk), which means 'building for storing salt'.

Place names can also indicate which animals were kept. Skipton (North Yorkshire) means 'sheep farm'; Swindon (Wiltshire), 'pig hill'; and Horsham (Sussex), 'horse village'.

Some names tell us about the local wildlife: Everton (Merseyside) means 'wild boar village'; Broxbourne (Hertfordshire), 'stream where badgers are found'; and Leixlip (Kildare), 'salmon leap'.

▲ Gatwick, Surrey, means 'goat farm', although the goats have now been replaced by jet aeroplanes.

Place names from ancient sites

Place names can guide archaeologists to ancient sites. Those containing the Old English word *hlaw* (such as Ludlow in Shropshire) or its plural, *hlaew* (as in Lewes, East Sussex), usually mean there was a burial mound (or mounds) there. Many burial mounds were built 2,000 or so years before the Saxons named the places, but they could obviously still be seen.

Other place names show where the Romans built their roads or forts.

The Old English name for a Roman road was *straet*. The names of Street (Somerset) and Stratford-upon-Avon (Warwickshire) tell us that these places were on, or near, a Roman road. The words *chester*, *caster* or *cester* come from the Old English word *caester* (which comes from the Latin *castra*), meaning 'fort'. The Roman fort at Chesterfield in Derbyshire was only found in recent years, but it was obvious it was there from the name.

Many places were built with defensive fortifications against attacks from unfriendly neighbours or invaders from overseas. Cashel in

Tipperary means 'circular stone fort', and Donegal means 'fort of the strangers' – in this case meaning the Vikings. The Saxons also protected their towns with banks and walls against attacks by the Vikings. Saxon place names ending in -burgh mean 'fortified place'. Bamburgh (Northumberland) means 'fortified place belonging to Bebba'. Bebba was the wife of the king of Northumbria.

Strange place names

Some places have names that make us laugh, though their original meanings may not be very funny at all:

Crackpot (N. Yorkshire)	Deep hole where crows gather.
Steeple Bumstead (Essex)	Place where reeds grow.
Great Snoring (Norfolk)	Homestead of a man called Snear.
Toller Porcorum (Dorset)	Hollow stream of the pigs.
Pity Me (Durham)	Little sea (from the French, *petite mer*).

▼ The church at Good Easter in Essex. This village's name has nothing to do with the Christian festival but simply means 'place by the sheep pen belonging to a woman called Godgyth'.

Religious place names

Christianity did not become the main religion of Britain until about the eighth century AD. Some place names tell us where earlier gods were worshipped. Tara (Meath) is named after a Celtic goddess called Temair, meaning 'the dark one'.

▲ Thor, the Viking god of thunder.

Baldock is Baghdad

The town of Baldock in Hertfordshire was founded in the twelfth century by the Knights Templar. They were a military and religious group of knights who tried to protect the holy Christian sites from invaders in what is now the Middle East. The Knights Templar named Baldock after Baldac, a Christian village in Arabia. Baldac later became Baghdad, which is now the capital of Iraq.

▶ This is what a Knight Templar looked like.

Wednesbury (West Midlands) is named after the Saxon god Woden (Wednesday comes from this too), and Thundersley (Essex) comes from Thor, the Viking god of thunder (Thursday is also named after him).

Egles, an old Celtic word for church, gives us the place name Eccles (Greater Manchester). Many places in Ireland and Scotland have names beginning with Kil- (from *cill*, another Celtic word for a church), such as Killybegs (Donegal), which means 'the little churches'.

The Welsh word for church is *llan* (pronounced something like hlan). Many Welsh place names start with Llan-, followed by the name of the saint to whom the church is dedicated. Llandudno (Gwynedd) means St. Tudno.

The Vikings called a church *kirkja*, which gives us Kirkham (village with a church) and Ormskirk (Orm's church), both in Lancashire. *Mynster* was the Anglo-Saxon word for a monastery or large church: Warminster (Wiltshire) means 'church on the River Were'.

▲ Lavenham, Suffolk, was famous for producing woollen cloth in the fifteenth century and contains many buildings which date from that time. The name means 'home of a man called Lafa'.

Places called after people

How would you like to be called Gurl, Eorp, Hwita or Wocc? These were the first names of some of our Saxon ancestors. We don't know anything about these people and we only know their names because they are part of place names. Gorleston-on-Sea (Norfolk) comes from Gurl, Arlingham (Gloucestershire) from Eorp, Whittingham (Northumberland) from Hwita, and Woking (Surrey) from Wocc.

When the Saxons arrived in England, they moved around the country in groups. The place where a group eventually settled might be known by the name of the group or its leader. Hitchin (Hertfordshire) means 'the territory of the Hicce tribe'. Hastings (East Sussex) means 'the territory of Haesta's people' (Haesta means the violent one).

The Normans, too, used personal names as place names, sometimes adding a surname to an existing name. The name Ashby-de-la-Zouch (Leicestershire) tells us that this particular Ashby (ash tree farm), one of several in the Midlands, belonged to the Zuche family. Leighton Buzzard (Buckinghamshire) means a leek farm (Leighton) belonging to someone called Theobald de Busar.

Clues from Names

Modern place names

Most places had been given their names by 1500, but some have since been renamed, and new villages and towns have been built.

Many places in Ireland were renamed by the English, who were trying to conquer Ireland from the twelfth century. Some of these names have been changed back into Irish. Dun Laoghaire, near Dublin, for example, was known as Kingstown from 1821 to 1920.

In Northern Ireland, where many English and Scottish families settled in the seventeenth century, English and Scottish names still survive, like Newtownards (County Down), meaning new town in the Ards peninsula, and Randalstown (County Antrim), from the first name of a Scottish earl.

▲ Ironbridge, Shropshire. The area takes its name from this famous bridge, built in 1779.

Several places in England have had another word added to their name, either to tell them apart from other places with the same name or to highlight something special about them. In 1582, Saffron became part of the name Saffron Walden (Essex) because saffron, a plant that gives us a food flavouring and colouring, was grown there. 'Spa' was added after the name Boston (Yorkshire) when mineral springs (believed to heal illnesses) were discovered there in 1744. Bognor took on the word Regis (which means 'of the king') to become Bognor Regis (West Sussex) after King George V went there to recover from an illness in 1929.

Llanfairpwllgwyngyllgogerychwyrndrobwl-

What a mouthful! This is the full name of a village in Anglesey (Gwynedd) and is the longest place name in Britain and Ireland.

It is thought to have been made up as a joke by a tailor who lived in the area in the nineteenth century. He took the village's original name and added the names of other places nearby.

The name means 'St. Mary's church in the hollow of the white

▲ Bournville near Birmingham was built in 1879 to house workers at Cadbury's chocolate factory.

In the nineteenth century, during the Industrial Revolution, new districts grew up to provide homes for the workers in the factories and mines. Wattstown (Mid Glamorgan) is named after Edmund Watts, who ran a coal mine. Port Sunlight (Merseyside) was built to house the workers at the Lever Brothers' factory, which made Sunlight soap.

Westward Ho! (Devon) is called after a book of the same name published in 1855. In the book, the author, Charles Kingsley, describes an area in Devon. The story was very popular, and local business people felt that tourists would be attracted to a resort with the same name. Westward Ho! is the only name in Britain and Ireland with an exclamation mark after it.

Peacehaven (Sussex) was named in 1917 when the First World War was coming to an end.

llandysiliogogogoch

hazel near the whirlpool and St. Tysilio's church by the cave'.

People generally shorten it to Llanfair PG, but the full name used to appear on the sign at the railway station and on the platform ticket, the longest platform ticket in the world.

Glossary

Ancestors The people from whom a person is descended; relatives from the distant past.

Anglicized Made to sound or look more English.

Aramaic An ancient language of the Middle East.

Archaeologists People whose job is to study ancient objects and remains to find out about what happened in history.

Classical A period of history dominated by the ancient Greeks and Romans.

Chronicles Records of events in history.

Curator Someone who looks after a museum.

Cycle A set period of time that repeats itself.

Earl A nobleman.

Expelled To be forced to leave.

Fortifications Walls or banks built to keep out enemies.

Hebrew An ancient language which comes from Israel.

Heroine The main female character in a story.

Huguenots A group of French Protestants in the seventeenth century.

Identify To recognize someone or something.

Immigrants People who have settled in a country that is not their own.

Industrial Revolution A period during the eighteenth and nineteenth centuries when factories were set up in Britain to make goods.

Inheritance Property or goods that are given to someone when the previous owner dies.

Medieval Of the Middle Ages.

Middle Ages The period in British history from 1066 to 1485.

Middle East The area around the eastern Mediterranean.

Muslim A person who believes in the religion of Islam.

New Testament A collection of books written soon after Christ's death and added to the Old Testament to make up the Christian Bible.

Old Testament The collection of books that make up the sacred scriptures of the Jews.

Pageant A colourful, elaborate parade or display acting out scenes from history.

Parish registers Books in which the births, deaths and marriages that happen in an area are written down.

Patron saint A saint considered to be the protector of a country.

Peninsula A narrow strip of land sticking out into a sea or lake.

Persecuted Treated badly, usually because of race or religion.

Plantation of Ulster The settling of English and Scottish people in Northern Ireland during the seventeenth century.

Population All the people living in a country.

Prophet A person chosen by God to teach people to believe in God's way of life.

Protestant A Christian person who does not accept the Pope as the Head of the Christian Church.

Reformation The move away from the Roman Catholic Church in countries of northern Europe including England, Scotland and Wales during the sixteenth century.

Sikh A person who believes in a religion from India that worships God.

Syllable One part of a word.

Translate To change something into a different language.

Tribe A group of families ruled by a chief.

Books to read

Younger children may need help in getting information from these books.

General books about names

Dunkling, L., *Guinness Book of Names* (Guinness Publishing, 1993)

Room, A. *Brewer's Dictionary of Names* (Cassell, 1992)

First names

Asante, M. K., *The Book of African Names* (Africa World Press, 1991)

Chuks-Orji, O., *Names from Africa* (Johnson Publishing, 1972)

Dunkling L. & Gosling W., *Everyman's Dictionary of First Names* (Dent, 1993)

Kamath, M. V., *Jaico Book of Baby Names* (Jaico Publishing House, 1987)

Nu'man, M. A., *Muslim Names and Their Meaning* (New Mind Productions, 1984)

Qazo, M. A., *What's in a Muslim Name?* (Kazi Publications, 1982)

Withycombe, E. G., *The Oxford Dictionary of English Christian Names* (Omega Books, 1988)

Surnames

Cottle, B., *The Penguin Dictionary of Surnames* (Penguin Books, 1978)

Freeman, J. W., *Discovering Surnames* (Shire Publications, 1973)

Hanks, P. & Hodges F., *A Dictionary of Surnames* (OUP, 1988)

McKinley, R. A., *A History of British Surnames* (Longman 1990)

Place names

Gelling, M. *Place Names in the Landscape* (Dent, 1993)

McDonald, F. & Cresswell, J., *The Guinness Book of British Place Names* (Guinness Publishing, 1993)

Mills, A. D., *A Dictionary of English Place Names* (OUP, 1991)

Nicolaisen, W. F. H., *Scottish Place-Names* (Batsford, 1976)

Room, A., *A Dictionary of Irish Place Names* (Appletree Press, 1986)

Room, A., *A Dictionary of Place Names in the British Isles* (Bloomsbury, 1988)

Index of names

The words in **bold** refer to pictures as well as text.

Index

The words in **bold** refer to pictures as well as text.